Faces of Fishing Creek

Kyle Laws

Middle Creek Publishing & Audio
Beulah, CO • USA

Faces of Fishing Creek
© **2018, Kyle Laws**

No part of this book may be reproduced by any means known at this time or derived henceforth without written permission of the publisher or author. The exception would be in the case of brief quotations embodied in the critical articles or reviews and pages where permission is specifically granted by the publisher or author.

Books may be purchased in quantity and/or special sales by contacting the publisher. All inquiries related to such matters should be addressed to:

Middle Creek Publishing & Audio
9027 Cascade Avenue
Beulah, CO 81023
editor@middlecreekpublishing.com
(719) 369-9050

Author Image: Penelope Hyland
Cover Design: David A. Martin,
Middle Creek Publishing
Printed in the United States

First Edition, 2018

ISBN: 978-0998932217

Faces of Fishing Creek

Kyle Laws

Contents

7   Preface

Clara and Joseph: 1926-1933

11   Clara: Bates, Descended of Whalers, Sells Me the First Section of Fishing Creek After Joseph's Failure at Woodbine, 1926
12   Clara: Anna Akhmatova Was Born 1889 in Odessa, Ukraine
13   Joseph Writes: Of Darkest Wildwood, 1927
14   Clara: New Year's Day, 1928
15   Joseph Writes: No Harm, 1928
16   Clara Writes: Leave, 1928
17   Joseph: Fire of the Day, 1929
18   Clara: Words Rise Up, 1930
19   Joseph: Of Winter, 1931
20   Clara Writes: Sins of the House, 1931
21   Joseph Writes: Off a Cliff of Shoals, 1932
22   Clara: Untidy and Unkempt, 1932
23   Clara: Returning to Stream, 1933
24   Clara: Whitesboro, 1933

Clara and Joseph: 1933-1939

29   Clara: Slow Waltz, 1933
30   Clara: This Likely Too Will Fail, 1933
31   Joseph: Seeking Asylum, 1935
32   Clara: I Look to the Sky, 1935
33   Joseph Writes: Before Dawn, 1936
34   Clara: Truth Be Told, 1937
35   Joseph: High Ground, 1937
36   Joseph: Turn to Me, 1938
37   Joseph Writes: In Order Alphabetic— Blackness, Bridge and Crow, 1939
38   Clara Writes: Winter's First Hard Freeze, 1939

Contents

Joseph: 1939-1958

43	Joseph: New Jersey Avenue, 1939
44	Joseph: Oysters, 1939
45	Joseph: By This Conveyance, 1939
46	Joseph: Changes in the Solidity of Ice, 1940
47	Joseph Writes: Fishing Creek, 1940
48	Joseph: Court House Diner, 1940
49	Joseph Writes: Two Pines, 1945
50	Joseph: Dilemma, 1948
51	Joseph: Starlings at the Window, 1955
52	Joseph: Legacy, 1958

Epilogue: Recollections of a Girl Growing Up in Fishing Creek

57	Sand and Muck, 1959
58	Rac•ism /ˈrāˌsizəm/ *n* a distinction based on color, 1960
59	Matthews: Family With 100% Historical Intermarriage to Other Whaler Yeomen, 1965
60	Cape May-Lewes Ferry Voyages, 2007
61	Returning to the Cape, 2009
62	To Joseph: After Reading All the Deeds With a Covenant Restricting Use to the Caucasian Race, 2013
63	I Remember Lessons in Grief, 2014
64	Debris-Strewn Beach, 2015

Preface

Faces of Fishing Creek is a novella in poems in the voices of two characters, Clara and Joseph, who developed an isolated section of southern New Jersey as a summer resort for Philadelphia residents.

The precursor to Fishing Creek was Town Bank, established about 1685 on the shores of the Delaware Bay for the industry of offshore whaling. After whaling ceased as a means of livelihood, the settlers became known as whaler yeomen when they established plantations between the creeks that flowed into the bay.

Until the twentieth century the area remained isolated. Thirty-five families controlled most of the area—property passing through intermarriage—when tracts of land began to be sold for a development called Wildwood Villas in 1926, later shortened to the Villas.

Abundant fish, which brought the whales, was touted in advertisements along with a notation that the community was restricted to the "white race." I grew up in the Villas in the 1950s and 1960s, did not know that the deed for every lot sold until 1958 contained this racial covenant.

Thoughts expressed by Clara and Joseph are the author's after researching land transfer deeds and newspaper articles. Recollections in the author's epilogue are my own after growing up in the village first known as Fishing Creek.

Kyle Laws

Clara and Joseph: 1926-1933

Clara: Bates, Descended of Whalers, Sells Me the First Section of Fishing Creek After Joseph's Failure at Woodbine, 1926

Bates thinks I traveled to this village like the tide over sand bars,
a long distance between high and low, coming from Odessa

to be a mask for Wildwood Villas, my name on the first tract,
each lot sold by my husband with a covenant

restricting use to "the white or Caucasian race."
I beg Joseph not to write the deeds that way as breezes blow

across the mudflats that smell of weakies, blues, and flounder
that will jump onto any baited hook.

I become a perpetual nag, a hag, while his brochures
extol the high ground of once-plantations, advertise bungalows

with four rooms and a porch, outdoor plumbing, artesian water,
and a lot—all as low as $300, payments taken.

Clara: Anna Akhmatova Was Born 1889 in Odessa, Ukraine

Odessa, where Joseph and I meet shopping for lace
on a narrow street,

tops of buildings where shopkeepers sleep leaning
to each other as trees.

I carry a book of Anna's poems.
Joseph says I can take her with me if I will leave.

He will bring Pushkin's *Eugene Onegin.*
And they will write to each other on mornings

washed by a sea like the quartz they call diamonds
gathered at Sunset Beach.

Joseph Writes: Of Darkest Wildwood, 1927

And our young poet — Olga fired him…
he fell in love with darkest wildwood

                Alexander Pushkin, *Eugene Onegin*,
                    Chapter Two, XXII

What I know of women, I learned from Pushkin.
What I know of Clara is that she's become
Olga and Tatyana, Onegin and Lensky,
characters Tchaikovsky made into opera.
And they never end happily.

She is one for whom dawn rises as spring catapults
to summer, as horseshoe crabs make their way to lay
eggs in the sand, as she carries sheaves of poetry
to the hull of a cabin cruiser wrecked and washed
up in a March nor'easter.

She will never attach to this shore in the way
she did her beloved Odessa. Never attach to me
as a wife should to husband. Her attraction to lost ships
hides an unhappiness with the place I've named Wildwood.
To all the world a success, but we silent and unsatisfied.

Clara: New Year's Day, 1928

       after Anna Akhmatova,"The Guest"

My brother whispers with Joseph in the dining room,
heads bent over the blond mahogany table and a plat

of the lots of Wildwood Villas. I mix drinks in the kitchen
from the Canadian Club brought in on Gabby's outboard,

the one used to pick up shipments intercepted by the Coast Guard,
same Guardsmen who drink at the saloon where Gabby tends bar,

where they talk about where cargo is dumped over drinks.
He serves them the same bootleg whiskey they think destroyed

by the winter rough of bay. We pretend we don't know, but do.
We think we've changed, but have not.

We think this new world is different from the old.
We think the waters of May we dip in—before the flush

of those escaping the cities—purifies us.
We think this covenant restricting use to the Caucasian race

is somehow not wrong, somehow the harbor of liberty
we sailed through on our way here.

Joseph Writes: No Harm, 1928

> *Her father…*
> *could see no harm in books; himself*
> *he never took one from the shelf,*
> *thought them a pointless peccadillo*
>
> Alexander Pushkin, *Eugene Onegin*,
> Chapter Two, XXIX

Harmless as the spear for hunting whale,
as the perch above the dune where the watcher
kept his watch for any show of water from a spout,
as the nor'easter in March that undermined shacks.

That way of life was almost gone along the bay
when Pushkin penned *Eugene Onegin*,
when that novel in verse changed our literature,
brought what happened in parlors, fields,

and coastlines onto the page in a language
everyone could understand, and then the stirrings
began, the dissatisfactions under the surface
like the submerged whale waiting for breath.

These once whalers, a kind of royalty,
will live with the common of cities in their escape.
Pushkin will take over where once Longfellow
was read by the light of oil, as I string wires
for electricity from bungalow to bungalow.

Clara Writes: Leave, 1928

> *Oh enchanting little town of riddles,*
> *Though I love you, I am mournful…*
>
> *But I don't like the hour before sunset,*
> *The wind from the sea and the word:* "Leave."
>
> Anna Akhmatova, "In Tsarskoye Selo, 1"

As I lie in bed alone,
listen to the lap, lap on shore,
this high tide a long way
across the ripple of sandbar,
I plot how I can live
in the swath of grass,
become the protrude of ears
of a fox in the dunes.

Today I walked south
below where whalers
first shacked and rendered
what was beneath the skin,
so up river they could light rooms,
the women mend and darn,
the men keep their account books.

I knew I had gone too far
when the bath of sun became a voice,
"You have overstayed your welcome."

Joseph: Fire of the Day, 1929

Brochures I send out as Christmas cards
extol sunsets equaled only by Key West.
No mention as a Jew I do not celebrate.

And when the globe dips into the bay,
it can be so quick, it makes me feel
as if this all could be taken away.

Not a little bit at a time
like the concrete ship Atlantus
split on the shoals at Sunset Beach.

But as the breath held when you fly
into the horizon, staring at a sun
you know not to, waiting for its fall.

Clara: Words Rise Up, 1930

The longer I'm here, the more our Russian words rise up
off the page and look back to the Black Sea of Odessa.

For it is Anna's poetry I read, hers the voice I hear.
There are no operas, ballets or symphonies by Tchaikovsky,

but a private world where I can dream who I want to be.
Instead of the street noise of trolleys, there's the chatter

of gulls as they swoop to follow fishing boats back to poles
where they tie up, rest at odd angles as if questioning

where they've been left—I the cocked motor pulled forward
into the slush of bay and gasoline in the bottom of the boat.

I wait for another tide as I pore over deeds in a language
just outside my reach. Are they telling me I can build

as far out as the flats lie bare at low water? Use stilts
to move closer to an opposing shore?

Joseph: Of Winter, 1931

It is always of winter that I write
because other seasons are full
of hammers and nails and cement
and lumber and shingles for roofs
and tubs and sinks and linoleum
over wooden floors.

When I have no money for the men,
they take their pay in lots
as there are always fish to catch
and chickens in the yards.
A few of my carpenters will be set
when this Depression ends,
should stay with me through
the good times as well.

Clara Writes: Sins of the House, 1931

> *Having forgiven me my sins, he fell silent.*
> Anna Akhmatova, "Confession"

My sins are of the house I do not hold as center,
the marriage not sacred, the children not my all.

I came to this gradually, nothing to tell me before
other than I was not charmed by dolls as other girls.

I spent most of my time outdoors, school where I did well,
not figuring out how to dress and wear my hair.

When I arrived from Odessa, women had cut their tresses,
wore shorter dresses—stocking seams and calves bared.

Hems fell along with markets of real estate and stock.
Now, back where we began, there's no other way

to get by honorably except marriage,
especially if you are born poor.

Joseph Writes: Off a Cliff of Shoals, 1932

> *Dear Tanya, you're condemned to perish;*
> *but first, the dreams that hope can cherish*
> *evoke for you a sombre bliss*
>
> > Alexander Pushkin, *Eugene Onegin,*
> > *Chapter Three, XV*

My dear Clara, something in your temperament
is provoked by these most desolate of winters,
where the wind off bay roars not far from the Atlantic,
over the deep channel off a cliff of shoals.

William Penn spent a season and —even that Quaker
in an escape from lands where beliefs were expected
to be similar—judged the harshness beyond what he
could weather and moved his fledgling colony up-river.

I worked any job I could, saved, and paid for passage
for my parents, you, and your brother.
I can make us a life in freedom unimaginable
from where we come, our country still torn from revolution.

A degree in agriculture from Cornell convinced
these yeoman whalers I could make them prosperous.
They had scraped out a living from what no one
since natives had wanted, guarding it as treasure.

Please stay as long as you can: I know what I'm doing.
This is the dream that came before the seeing.
This is the prescience of vision my feet knew
as soon as they stepped onto these shores.

Clara: Untidy and Unkempt, 1932

I could walk on Bayshore Road, but keep to the beach,
untidy and unkempt as I am becoming.

I could go beyond the boundaries of creek,
but would have to walk out onto sandbars

at low tide where Fishing Creek flows into the bay,
or wade with my skirt held high at Coxe Hall Creek,

both hard to do in the winter bite that blows
fourteen miles from Delaware.

I am bounded, lonely, not able to make friends
among the poor who live in bungalows

never meant for other than summer fishing.
I will tell Joseph he must teach me to drive.

He will if I tell him I have taken to talking to gulls,
reading poetry into the wind.

One gull likes Anna Akhmatova as much as I do,
lifts his wings, caws, resettles when I get to a favorite.

I wish my husband listened as closely.
Instead he builds houses for those who cannot pay.

Clara: Returning to Stream, 1933

The Consolidated School in Cold Spring needs a French
and German teacher. I have applied.

I will ride to school with the children of town if Joseph
cannot find me a car. It's that, or I have to leave.

I know this is his dream, and I thought it was mine too,
an Odessa in America.

But this is no cosmopolitan port city where I learned
languages from across the world.

Schellenger Landing sailors stumble on their English tongues
as if the language were not their own.

I prefer the whistle at noon that reminds me it's Wednesday.
And it's time I stopped these thoughts

because I might convince myself I do not belong, and I do.
I was meant to be here from the first time I saw Joseph

on that crowded city street. My feet have learned these tide lines
as if I were born in the estuary of Fishing Creek,

as if I swam out into the bay with my first blood,
as if I were a salmon returning to its stream.

Clara: Whitesboro, 1933

I haven't told Joseph, but tomorrow I will drive
to Whitesboro to find a maid, someone to cook,

clean, and care for our daughters while I work.
Consolidated School has hired me.

I laugh when I hear my oldest in conversation
with a neighbor who asks what religion we are,

and she replies, "Consolidated." I like her answer.
Here, it is your school that defines who you are.

It's a barb in my husband's side for me to hire
a black maid. But there's so little I know about

the people who once were slaves. Whitesboro,
named after one of Booker T. Washington's

lawyers, was designed for Southern blacks
to escape persecution, but also for black workers

in the hotels and boarding houses of local resorts.
And if I'm Akhmatova and Joseph is Pushkin,

I want to understand those whom we've excluded
from Wildwood Villas, and a country that would

have Pushkin, descended of an African prince,
live in a town called Whitesboro.

Clara and Joseph: 1933-1939

Clara: Slow Waltz, 1933

>after Anna Akhmatova, "We are all carousers and loose women here..."

School starts Monday.
This, my celebration,
this, after Canadian Club.

I rock my hips inside a skirt
loose from walking
the sand at tide line,

twirl up on toes,
arches high from the cup
of what gives under feet,

extend hands above head
as if swimming against
the gentle current of bay.

You leave the chair by the fire,
take the pipe from your lips,
bring them to mine.

We glide across wood
to the bedroom door,
a slow waltz.

Clara: This Likely Too Will Fail, 1933

> *He spoke of the summer, and he also said*
> *That for a woman to be a poet was—absurd.*
>
>   Anna Akhmatova, "We met for the last time…"

I am chattering as a crow in early morning
or sparrows in the pine at dusk.

Out of nowhere, Joseph says that for a woman
to teach German and French

is absurd. As if he's been reading Anna.
I snap back that it's not the Depression

slowing sales, but his own bad luck.
This development likely too will fail

as Woodbine did—not that long ago
or far as the kestrel wings across creeks.

I do this in both German and French,
not sure if he can follow.

"At least they're going to pay me,"
I shout as I slam the door.

He afraid of losing me.
Me afraid teaching won't work.

Joseph: Seeking Asylum, 1935

Mornings, I rise late, Clara already gone to school.
I find her letters on the kitchen table,
letters we write to each other every day
even though we could as well talk.

They are in French, a language she writes
better than Russian. I pull the dictionary hidden
in a drawer under the table because she asks
to see translations in both Russian and English.

I am her best student, the one to whom she can write
what she cannot say, what she cannot be on a peninsula
at the end of a state, at the end of a journey,
we, pilgrims seeking asylum in the quiet of trees.

Clara: I Look to the Sky, 1935

The longer I'm here, the more I study the sky.
It's not just the shorebirds that migrate in spring,

but hawks, eagles, and osprey. And songbirds
—cardinals, blue jays, red-winged blackbirds,

and the humble sparrows. I look up because
I have my own wings—a little outboard and

motor that slaps, slaps as I hurry down
the bay to Higbee's Beach where the dunes

are prominent with all species of plants.
The birds gather there, this, on the flight path

from South America to the Arctic for some,
the beach one of the last that resembles what

the whalers first saw. From May to November,
I take a blanket, spread it in the slope of sand

between one dune and another after pulling
the boat up on shore. I listen for a song

or screech, and when a rustle comes from the holly,
I shoot with camera. I will record all there is

about this most desolate place, this place like
nowhere else on earth, a haven my husband

found and called his own, as all the generations
of yeoman whalers before.

Joseph Writes: Before Dawn, 1936

> *and when, by misty moon, the east*
> *is softly, indolently sleeping,*
> *wakened at the same hour of night*
> *Tatyana'd rise by candlelight.*
>
>   Alexander Pushkin, *Eugene Onegin*,
>   Chapter Two, XXVIII

My Clara awakens before dawn,
when she hears the rustle of the fox,
when the first gulls begin to call,
when men untie their boats from poles
as the tide moves in.

As if floating in the mouth of the bay where salt
balances fresh, she arches her back and stretches
to welcome the day. This, how she welcomes me—
to the clatter of a fishing village about its work
as if nothing has changed in 200 years.

Waters where whalers once hunted from boats
as small as those to rescue the errant from undertows.
But Clara knows the currents well enough to swim
at the edge of sleep. And I have learned to embrace
what fades like a moon as the sun rises through leaves.

Clara: Truth Be Told, 1937

Truth be told, I like my life on the coast
of the Delaware Bay, the quiet of winter,

the carnival of summer in a village not far
from Wildwood, resort on the Atlantic,

beach littered with horseshoe crabs, archaic creatures
that lumber out of waves to lay eggs.

Bound to the land as generations who scraped a living
out of cranberry bogs, wool milled from sheep,

apple orchards, and the fertilizer harvested
from crabs that did not make it back from shore,

I have a freedom I could not know elsewhere,
that I crossed an ocean for.

Yeoman whalers protected this paradise of coastal land,
all the fish they could eat,

welcomed us as those can who know things change,
seeing us as their best bet.

And I walk the beaches, missing the gardens of Odessa,
but not the famine of the revolutionary years.

Joseph: High Ground, 1937

Clara listens to women from the old families,
the outcasts, the ones who drift like buoys
gone from their moorings, the ones who live
in my bungalows in winter—too many children,
fathers hard to track.

Clara asks where they were before I carved out
lots for houses on the Cape. They have always
been here, but not as peasants without masters.
The dreams I sold for escape from the hardship
of city attracted every young unhappy woman.

And she left family and prospects with dowry
for a life different from marrying someone
known since she was a child. She thought
the summer boy would stay the winter,
would find a way to make a living.

Each one left after Labor Day, and by spring
there was a child of hope. Ten years of hope
created an underclass who know this land
better than I ever will with my discussions
of high ground and drainage ditches.

Joseph: Turn to Me, 1938

We rarely talk about fall,
only the hot extreme of summer
or the bold coldness of winter.
But fall goes on till mid-November,

the surf warm and strong with smell
of fish gone uncaught in the bay.
A place to swim, but we rarely do,
tired of the stuff of tourists.

Clara, join me today, this late
October, for a swim in the bay.
Walk to the end of the pier
down from Fishing Creek,

boundary of our world.
Dive out over the ripple of wave
as the tide rolls in, your belly
skimming the top as if a stone

across the surface of pond.
Turn to me, I'm right behind.
Share your lover, this Odessa
on the shores of South Jersey.

Joseph Writes: In Order Alphabetic—
Blackness, Bridge and Crow, 1939

> *Tatyana's haunted by her vision,*
> *plagued by her ghastly dream*
>
> Alexander Pushkin, *Eugene Onegin,*
> *Chapter Five, XXIV*

Clara does not know all the stories
of those who've died on these shores,
but she thinks something
makes for such dramatic tides,
something never meant to be tamed,
something in the rustle of crows' wings,
something that unsettles her dreams.

She is wed to this landscape
and that which came before seeps
in like the perpetual burn of sun and wind.
And the only way the sea knows to keep
what it loves is to envelop it in a storm.
I am jealous of this union, fearful for her.
There's a passage between shoals
the old timers know, but you cannot
have started sail into the mouth of the bay.
Tomorrow I will tell her.

Clara Writes: Winter's First Hard Freeze, 1939

> *The willow spreads its transparent fan…*
> *Perhaps I should not have become*
> *Your wife.*
>
>   Anna Akhmatova, "The heart's memory of the sun grows faint…"

Not willow, but mimosa
on sides of an unpaved Delaware Parkway
named in the first deed.

Not champagne and orange juice
served on Sunday,
but pink fronds on Wednesday.

This, our re-creation of a bathing resort
on the Black Sea. This, what you promised.
What I have come to love more than our union.

How could I have known
there'd be something in the night breeze,
something that would come between,
something more than our children I will leave.

Something that could be faith—
the way wind sweeps up the bay in row
upon row of frozen waves as far as I can see
as if a god's hand stopping them from their fall.

Joseph: 1939-1958

Joseph: New Jersey Avenue, 1939

I fall. Trip on the top step of a porch
and lie sprawled against the door.
Drawings for a new model scatter across boards
not yet painted a battleship grey that gives
the cottages a marine feel—subtle, inexpensive.
Tears roll down my face at the misstep.

I measure the risers,
the top one off, the carpenter wrong.
I built this backwater into a town
from the shoreline to the other side
of the dirt road through Fishing Creek.
I wanted Clara to know she'd chosen well.

Joseph: Oysters, 1939

On Sunday afternoons, I go to the Lobster House,
sit at a table along windows onto the dock,
order oysters. First one half dozen, then another,
chat with the waitress about a third. The staff
remember the ritual of Clara and me, and ask
as if on cue if I have room for the entrée.

The red and white checked tablecloth is littered
with garlic and sesame seeds from crusty bread.
I only eat a few bites of the flounder even though
the crabmeat stuffing is best just out of the oven.
I ask them to box it up, put Clara's order in to go—
pretending she's still with me a few more weeks.

Joseph: By This Conveyance, 1939

I'm hearing reports of Germany,
the Night of Crystal a beginning.
Russian pogroms all over again.
Clara's gone—the one I could talk to.

She argued we were doing some of the same.
As long as we could discuss it back and forth,
there was the possibility of change.
The deeds, what do I do about the deeds?

"No part of the premises covered by this conveyance
shall ever be used or occupied for a dwelling
or any other purpose by any person or persons
other than those of the white or Caucasian race."

I'm stuck. The world is changing.
The one on whom I could rely is dead
as if by my own hand, by this town
where she died for lack of medical care.

Joseph: Changes in the Solidity of Ice, 1940

It was not death that I thought would take Clara,
but boredom, ennui, or the depression that descends
on those of northern climates. We are not that far north,
but winters can be like some gulag off the Black Sea,
wind bitter beyond imagination.

There were times I thought my face would crack
as I gazed onto the bay frozen to horizon, the freeze
not a neat pond, but the rough and tumble of wind-
whipped waves. We would cross it with our girls
on sleds out to the channel for ships.

But we never worried about collapse, falling in,
because it took heavy engines and bows to cut
the ice. We would see the surface freeze up behind
as soon as they passed and I wondered if this were
enough for Clara, these changes in the solidity of ice.

Joseph Writes: Fishing Creek, 1940

>*Or unconsoled by the returning*
>*of leaves that autumn killed for good,*
>*are we recalled to grief still burning*
>*by the new whisper in the wood?*
>
>   Alexander Pushkin, *Eugene Onegin*,
>   *Chapter Seven, III*

A year since Clara's death,
sudden, inexplicable, a turn of season
told by the change in light.

She woke with a pain in the night
cramped in our bed, called out
as I smoked a cigar on the porch.

I got her to the car where she lay
in the back seat while we roared
around curves of dirt roads,

crossed Delaware River Bridge
to arrive at Jefferson Hospital.
But her appendix had burst

on some unpaved Indian trail,
poison flowing through her body
like effluent from the fulling mill

where they processed the wool of sheep,
where I walk the woods of Fishing Creek
as if in the dense of oaks Clara might appear.

Joseph: Court House Diner, 1940

I sit in the same section every morning,
talk to the waitress as if I'm talking to Clara,
tell her my plans for the day,
how the construction is going.
She's begun to make suggestions.
She knows my children's names,
asks how they are doing in school.

I've offered the house, larger than we need,
to begin a hospital. If one had been here,
Clara might not have died.
This place has become my life and her death.
If I could take it back, I would.
But this is what I know; this is where we began,
where our children were born, and where I will die.

I will do it as I did before her death,
selling to Philadelphians who want to escape to the shore,
bringing their fears with them, as if having to live
beside those who picked cotton and tobacco in fields
is the worst that can happen to them.

They never would have survived our revolution,
never could have marched with little left of boots
across frozen fields, never could survive
even a winter of snow on the Delaware Bay.

Joseph Writes: Two Pines, 1945

> *Left-handed from the habitation*
> *where dwelt this child of inspiration,*
> *two pines have tangled at the root;*
> *beneath, a brook rolls its tribute*
>
> Alexander Pushkin, *Eugene Onegin,*
> *Chapter Six, XL*

Our town, now called only Villas,
is bordered by Fishing Creek,
an estuary spread between reeds
where minnows flit on the surface
and below crustaceans grow before
leaving for the wider bay.

What is disgorged in a roll of wave
does not return, but seeks its own life
even if tangled in seaweed and saltgrass
between the rise of bars where the oyster
is exposed, then closes its shell—Clara's,
open from the time she dwelled
in this village south of a forest of pine.

We were two twined against nor'easters,
roots deeper than reeds in the runoff.
We bloomed as a prickly pear in the dunes
for a short while. Then its fruit closed
in a deep red fist, waiting for the osprey
to spread wing, for the creek to purge itself
at the beginning of day.

Joseph: Dilemma, 1948

A birthday party. I'm at the end of the table.
Across from me sits one of Clara's friends
and her husband. Israel just created, the husband
has plenty to say. Then, he switches topics,

reveals the reason he quit smoking—
the Missouri president who put a special
tax on cigarettes, excluding the kind 80%
of blacks smoke—menthols, Kools,

what Nat King Cole uses for his voice.
"It's a racial tax, against whites, Missouri
still trying to backpedal being a slave state
during the war." This, as if it were yesterday.

Behind us, a black man sits at a table.
I don't know if he heard. I want to hide.
I've listened to a lot of this talk before.
No one ever says anything to the husband.

If I do, he'll bring up the covenant
against blacks living in the Villas.
But this has gone too far.
Still, I'm afraid of fracturing the group.

If I confront him, I may have to leave.
And they've been my stalwarts with Clara gone.

Joseph: Starlings at the Window, 1955

In my study, wings of starlings
bat at the Virginia Creeper tendriled
to screens over glass, no place to affix feet
for the last berries.

It's the sound of late fall, early winter.
By spring, sparrows, narrower, more compact,
not as black as the starlings will have stripped
the vine bare.

The circular drive of our house exits
onto a once-dirt thoroughfare, Clara,
like the goddess in the center garden, gone.
I never found anyone who could compare.

I will plant more vines, starlings, protest
those who cut trees so you do not roost.
I will find a place in what is left that I began,
somewhere for you on the Delaware Bay.

Joseph: Legacy, 1958

Warm, even with windows open and a breeze off the bay.
My stomach feels queasy. My arm goes numb.
I wrote a deal today for a couple from Conshohocken, PA.

Last month, the transfer to Bowman Builders
contained a statement they insisted upon—
"Restriction contained in deeds has been declared
unenforceable by Federal Courts of the United States."
He would not take the remaining lots without it.
I can tell everyone Bowman demanded it, a gracious way out.

Oh no, today's closing,
I think I used the old forms, covenant still there.
My legacy. Not all the work done to change.
A pain shoots across my chest.

Epilogue:
Recollections of a Girl
Growing Up in Fishing Creek

Sand and Muck, 1959

In between each sandbar out to low tide
where pearl-less oysters grow on the bay
is the black mud that children call muck.
The brave ones, the ones used to the debris
of tide and the unsettled wings of sandpipers,
walk through the valleys that spread black
between toes, raise legs as if a dinosaur leaving
tracks in ancient river beds, place the next
foot down until the rise of the ripple of sand.
We who live in the Villas are used to opposites—

The quiet of winter, the hustle of summer,
the town of 500 after the season, the resort of 3,000,
commercial fishermen and women shucking clams,
two weeks of vacation when Philadelphia factories
shut down for repairs and workers flood cheap rentals.
We house, feed in fish shacks, and serve in taprooms.
They cross to the other side of the peninsula for beaches
and amusement piers. No one ever swims here.
They drive to the ocean, afraid of the muck,
the dark between sandbars.

Rac•ism /ˈrāˌsizəm/ *n* a distinction based on color, 1960

My Irish grandfather plumbed the Philadelphia Sealtest Dairy
with black non-union workers, a former boxer striding
through picket lines with two burly men on either side,
        knowing there was nothing picketers
        could do without being called racist.

How a master plumber bid the job, kept costs down,
pipes holding up through five processing companies
and 65 years, although Grandfather did not.
        Stresses and conflicts led to his decline
        into blindness.

He kept it secret that his step-mother was a Native American
raised as mulatto in the Carolinas when he retired
to a "Caucasian only" fishing village on the bay,
        the least expensive place to live
        with water views.

We played in the white sand that was our front yard
under eyes that could no longer distinguish any variation
in color, only see the outline of figures
        dressed in bright madras shorts
        as we waved to him in the sun.

The story about the black workers always ended with
"They all came to the house on Sundays to eat."
I still don't know if Grandfather was a racist,
        or gave good jobs to labor
        that was cheapest.

Matthews: Family With 100% Historical Intermarriage to Other Whaler Yeomen, 1965

Carved out of land between Sarah Matthews on the south,
William Bates on the north, and the Delaware Bay on the west,
my town became Wildwood Villas, once part of plantations
and farms spread around Fishing Creek.

Carol Matthews was my friend through grade school.
I did not know her father was descended from the original
35 families of Lower Township, whalers turned yeomen
after the port of Town Bank was absorbed by the bay,
coastline shifting with the tides.

I would stay overnight with her when we got to 6th grade,
ride the school bus home to her father's gas station
on Route 9, wake to the ding of the line spread from office
to pumps as he ate breakfast between customers.
We slept upstairs under low slats of local cedar.

On Saturday, we'd walk down the side road with a name
of one of the families who'd always lived there,
climb onto a white horse, two or three of us,
ride bareback through fields stubbled after harvest.
This was before I knew her to be a kind of royalty.

I only knew her father's grease stained hands, and
her mother as she stood cooking at a big black stove.

Cape May-Lewes Ferry Voyages, 2007

First time I left the shore was 1964,
inaugural voyage of the ferry to Lewes, Delaware.
There had been a ferry before to Lewes, to Philadelphia.
The Atlantus, concrete ship from the First World War
was to be a dock, but it sank not far from the whalers'
first shacks on the bluff above the bay.

The sea where bay and ocean meet, the currents,
have their way with men, with women, with ships,
with the lighthouse, that beacon that rounds,
reflects off the low clouds at dusk and dawn
that illuminate the fox in the dunes
and the owl in tall cedars.
This is what I am afraid to leave
even though I'm booked for the return.
Mother did not cross with us.
She had to work that day.

She never wanted to leave by ferry after that.
Not while she was alive.
More than forty years go by.
I would like to say we scatter her,
but in actuality we toss her from the back
where cars settle in, mufflers silent,
still a scent of gasoline as gulls caw,
the ones they tell us not to feed.

My brother, experienced in burials at sea,
a Merchant Marine, tosses the black
garbage-like bag of ashes over in one sling.
I want to unloosen the tie as soon as it is gone,
so that somehow she can drift closer to the shore
neither one of us ever wanted to leave.

Returning to the Cape, 2009

A friend, indulging me by sailing back and forth
on the ferry in one afternoon, hurries to the table
with a local ale to tell me the woman behind the counter
butchers deer. I chuckle, explain what it was like
in the 50s and 60s, how the town I'm from is still known
for single mothers, or as the joke I heard on the ferry goes,

> *What holiday is not celebrated in the Villas?*
> *Father's Day. There are none.*

My friend introduces me as having grown up here.
I ask the butcher where she's from. She says, "Erma."
I ask what years she went to Consolidated School.
She would have been in my high school graduating class
had I stayed. And yes, she graduated,
which I was trying hard not to ask. I ask her name.
She's from one of the oldest families on the Cape.

I tell my friend how rough those years were
when everyone left on Labor Day and didn't return
until Memorial Day, except for the locals who'd been here
for generations, and single women with children
who had no other place to go like Mother, my sister,
and me. And how left alone for nine months,
we developed an appreciation for the landscape,
a love of the land I have never lost.

To Joseph: After Reading All the Deeds With a Covenant Restricting Use to the Caucasian Race, 2013

If I called you segregationist,
would you say, "The flounder with its white flesh
is different from the blue with its dark oiliness."

If I called you oppressor, would you tell me,
"Every policeman, fireman, and machinist
in Philadelphia feared losing his job
to the migration that started in cotton fields
and wound its way north.
It was their boil, my salve."

If I called you opportunist, would you answer,
"There were reasons I left a homeland,
took a degree in Agriculture at Cornell,
drifted south to New Jersey through Vineland
with row after row of grapes.
There was something about the whalers
who became farmers in the sand and bogs
I understood.
Something about the trees never cleared
for two hundred years.
Something about the oysters that flourished
in the murky bay."

I Remember Lessons in Grief, 2014

The house at the top
of New Jersey Avenue is gone.
All that's left are two graves
in the town of Cape May Court House.

Grandmother's wooden cross is gone.
The metal marker on the wedge for Grandfather
remains, between two cement planters
with embossed shells.

The shells dig their way into grass
like clams clamoring for the bottom
from hands placed on top
as first Grandmother,
then Mother, genuflected,
fell more than once,
sprawled like a blanket of evergreen
over Grandfather's grave.

Here I learned grief.
I came to know it to be as deep
as the artesian well
at the top of New Jersey Avenue.
There is nothing I cannot imagine
being done in its name.

Debris-Strewn Beach, 2015

I used to love the debris-strewn beach below Smitty's Bar
where run-off from beer mixed with the brackish tide.

I used to love the street names—
New York, New Jersey, Pennsylvania,
Bates (after one the land was transferred from),
Delaware Parkway, continuing on to cities, not states.

I used to love the bus that picked me up
on Bayshore Road in front of the Villas 5 & 10,
stock and cashier unchanged from the time of my birth
to its closing, the owner, Gracie, and the cashier, Cora,
friends and neighbors all their lives.

I used to love the round of bend after Fishing Creek
and how at Del Haven we took a hard turn, balancing
on the bus's wooden bench on the way to Green Creek.

Out there among the reeds, life began for those with a shell
and those without became fodder for whales.
And even though I know I should not, I still love the Villas,
embarrassingly flawed.

Notes

Anna Akhmatova translations are from *Selected Poems of Anna Akhmatova,* translated by Judith Hemschemeyer, edited and introduced by Roberta Reeder, Zephyr Press, Brookline, MA, 2000.

Alexander Pushkin translations are from *Eugene Onegin,* translated by Charles Johnston, The Viking Press, New York, 1978.

Title of the poem "Rac•ism /ˈrāˌsizəm/ *n* a distinction based on color, 1960" was inspired by *M•A•C•N•O•L•I•A,* A. Van Jordan, W.W. Norton & Company, New York, 2004.

Title of the poem "Matthews: Family With 100% Historical Intermarriage to Other Whaler Yeomen, 1965" is taken from a chart in *Cape May County, New Jersey,* Jeffery M. Dorwart, Rutgers University Press, New Brunswick, NJ, 1992, p. 275.

Acknowledgments

Grateful acknowledgment to the following publications where these poems first appeared, some in earlier versions and under different titles:

Abbey: "I Remember Lessons in Grief, 2014"

Chiron Review: "Matthews: Family With 100% Historical Intermarriage to Other Whaler Yeomen, 1965"

Lummox 4 Poetry Anthology 2015 (Lummox Press): "Cape May-Lewes Ferry Voyages, 2007"

Lummox 5 Poetry Anthology 2016 (Lummox Press): "Rac•ism /ˈrāˌsizəm/ n. a distinction based on color, 1960"

Misfit Magazine: "Joseph Writes: Off a Cliff of Shoals, 1932" and "Clara: Whitesboro, 1933"

Philadelphia Poets: "Returning to the Cape, 2009"

Visitant: "Clara: Bates, Descended of Whalers, Sells Me the First Section of Fishing Creek After Joseph's Failure at Woodbine, 1926,"
"Clara: Anna Akhmatova Was Born 1889 in Odessa, Ukraine,"
"Joseph Writes: Of Darkest Wildwood, 1927,"
"Clara: New Year's Day, 1928,"
"Joseph Writes: No Harm, 1928,"
"Clara Writes: Leave, 1928,"
"Clara: Words Rise Up, 1930,"
"Clara Writes: Sins of the House, 1931,"
"Clara: Returning to Stream, 1933,"

"Clara: This Likely Too Will Fail, 1933,"
"Joseph: Seeking Asylum, 1935,"
"Joseph Writes: Before Dawn, 1936," and
"Clara Writes: Winter's First Hard Freeze, 1939"

Waymark: "Joseph: Dilemma, 1948" and "Sand and Muck, 1959"

The author would also like to thank the Massachusetts Museum of Contemporary Art (MASS MoCA) for a residency where she worked on these poems and the Boiler House Poets in residency there for their valuable insights.

About The Author

Kyle Laws is based out of the Arts Alliance Studios Community in Pueblo, CO. Her previous collections include *This Town: Poems of Correspondence* with Jared Smith (Liquid Light Press, 2017); *So Bright to Blind* (Five Oaks Press, 2015); *Wildwood* (Lummox Press, 2014); *My Visions Are As Real As Your Movies, Joan of Arc Says to Rudolph Valentino* (Dancing Girl Press, 2013); and *George Sand's Haiti* (co-winner of Poetry West's 2012 award). With six nominations for a Pushcart Prize, her poems and essays have appeared in magazines and anthologies in the U.S., U.K., and Canada. Granted residencies in poetry from the Massachusetts Museum of Contemporary Art (MASS MoCA), she is one of eight members of the Boiler House Poets who perform and study at the museum. She is the editor and publisher of Casa de Cinco Hermanas Press.

Middle Creek Publishing Titles

Span
by David Anthony Martin

Deepening the Map
by David Anthony Martin

Phases
by Erika Moss Gordon

Cirque & Sky
by Kathleen Willard

*Messiah Complex and
Other Stories*
by Michael Olin-Hitt

*Lessons from Fighting
The Black Snake
at Standing Rock*
by Nick Jaina and Leslie Orihel

Wild Be
by One Leaf

Bijoux
by David Anthony Martin

Sawhorse
by Tony Burfield

*Almost Everything,
Almost Nothing*
by KB Ballentine

Across the Light
by Bruce Owens

I
Bengt O Björklund

Kimono Mountain
by Mike Parker

Paleos
Hoag Holmgren

Faces of Fishing Creek
by Kyle Laws

**No Better Place:
A New Zen Primer**
Hoag Holmgren

www.ingramcontent.com/pod-product-compliance
Lightning Source LLC
Chambersburg PA
CBHW062121080426
42734CB00012B/2945